I0026820

Poetic Philosophy Presents

Narrative Translations Designed For Accessibility

Beyond Good and Evil:

An Overture to a New Philosophy

By Jason Kassel, PhD

© 2025

Recursive Publishing

Table of Contents

⫘ Prelude: Why Vorspiel as "Overture" Matters

Nietzsche called this book a Vorspiel—a word often translated as *Prelude*. But in German, *Vorspiel* is not a preface. It is an overture: a musical or theatrical opening that introduces themes without explaining them. It plays before the play, not outside it.

In the 19th century, Nietzsche's readers would have heard this. *Vorspiel* meant Wagner. It meant rising tension, conflicting motifs, unresolved chords. The overture was not an introduction. It was a gesture of becoming.

In the 21st century, the word *Prelude* has dulled. It sounds polite. It sounds like background. But *Overture* still carries weight. It signals drama, performance, and theme before theory. In an era shaped by music, nonlinear media, and fluid identity, Nietzsche's tone feels more like a concept album than a treatise. He does not lead with clarity—he leads with sound and mask and tension.

This translation calls the book an Overture because Nietzsche isn't writing *about* philosophy. He is composing the possibility of a philosophy yet to come— through voice, through rhythm, through refusal. Like an overture, this book introduces themes it never resolves. Like Nietzsche himself, it begins again and again, without ever concluding.

To read this book is not to learn a system. It is to enter a space where thinking becomes performance.

Where   truth   dances.

Where   masks   speak.

Where the future begins as sound.

📖 Vorrede (Preface)

They call it love of truth. But most philosophers have simply feared lies— or their own shadow.

They set traps and wait for "certainty." But even certainty wears a mask.

They call it "objectivity." But what if the will to truth is only another form of desire?

What if truth is not pure? What if it is a woman? And man— just another seducer?

We have believed in God.
We have believed in grammar.
And so we have believed
that thought must be law,
that logic can save.

But now the wind shifts.
The sea returns.
And we—
the ones who breathe salt and silence—
must ask again:

Who dares to know?
Who dares to stand where the gods vanished?
Who dares to say:
I do not need certainty—
only rhythm?

This is no beginning.
This is the unmasking.

§1 – The Philosophers Want Ground

Philosophers want ground.
They want something firm
beneath their feet.

They say:
Truth must be still.
Truth must be one.
Truth must be good.

But who gave them these musts?
Who said truth must be moral?

Every "first principle"
hides a last fear.
Every system
is a disguised confession.

These thinkers
do not seek truth—
they defend their instincts
with logic.

---

§2 – The Free Spirit Has No Homeland

Even   the   freest   thinker
is not free from himself.

His   style—
his   rhythm—
his   metaphors—
they   all   expose   the   ground
he pretends to transcend.

Every   philosophy
is   a   portrait.
Every   truth
has a body.

---

§3 – The Instinct That Argues

To   think   is   to   mask   instinct.
To prove is to disguise desire.

Some   men   argue   for   "truth"
but kneel before what feels right.

The   mouth   says   "God."
The blood says "power."

---

§4 – The Will to System

"I only believe in a system
I can carry in my hand,"
someone said.

But what if that hand
is already trembling?

Philosophers build temples
out of fear.
They carve altars
to hide the abyss.

---

§5 – The Moral Bias

Why is it always
the good,
the true,
the rational,
the one?

Why does no one ask
if falsehood is fertile?

Philosophy fears contradiction.
But life
laughs in paradox.

---

§6 – Against Causal Arrogance

We   worship   causes.
We   say: A   leads   to   B.
But   our   "therefore"
is just a superstition in disguise.

We   cannot   stop   asking   why.
But the why often lies.

Our   cause   is   often
just   what   came   first
in   the   story
we   tell   ourselves
after.

---

§7 – Against Consciousness

Consciousness   is   late.
It   is   not   the   flame.
It is the smoke.

Our   deepest   thoughts
are   silent.
Our   truest   acts
happen without us.

The   ego   is   a   flare—
not the fire.

§8 – Language is the Old Lie

We   think   with   words.
But words come from the herd.

Our   grammar   teaches   us
that   there   must   be   doers
behind deeds.

So   we   invent
souls   behind   actions,
selves behind thoughts.

But   maybe   there   is
only   doing.
Only dancing.

§9 – The Subject is a Fiction

We   say: I   think.
But   what   if   that   "I"
is   a   story   the   thought   tells
about itself?

Thinking   happens.
But   the   thinker

is   only   a   shadow
cast by the verb.

---

§10 – The Philosopher's Puppet Show

We   call   it   "free   will,"
but   behind   the   curtain
stands   fear,   fatigue,
herd instinct.

We   are   not   puppeteers.
We are the strings.

The   noble   thinker
knows   the   hand   is   not   his.
He   learns   to   listen
to what moves him.

---

§11 – The Philosophical Temper

The   philosopher
does   not   ask:
What is true?

He   asks:
What   is   fruitful?

11

What gives shape
to becoming?

Even his deepest logic
is a child
of his temperament.

Truth is not found—
it is grown
from soil
he does not name.

---

§12 – The Doctrine of Opposites

Good and evil.
True and false.
Being and nothing.

We think in opposites
because we fear the in-between.

But life
does not draw lines.
It pulses.

Reality moves
in gradients and curves—
not borders.

§13 – The Will to Truth Conceals a Will to Power

The drive for truth
is not pure.
It is not neutral.

It demands,
it reshapes,
it kills what resists.

Behind "truth"
often crouches
the will to conquer.

To ask:
What is true?
is to ask:
What can be made
to kneel?

---

§14 – The Philosopher as Interpreter of Dreams

The philosopher dreams.
Then he awakens
and writes a system.

But   he   does   not   confess
  the dream.

He   carves   meaning
  from   fog—
  and calls it law.

---

§15 – Philosophy as the Most Subtle Confession

Every   philosophy
  is a secret biography.

Every   truth
  is a body's echo.

Philosophy   is   not   love   of   wisdom.
  It   is   the   wisdom   of
  what   one   fears,
  what   one   longs   for,
  what   one   cannot   name
  except sideways.

---

§16 – The Instinctual Philosopher

The   philosopher
  does   not   always   know
  what he's doing.

He   feels.
  He   orients.
  He   seeks   warmth—
  not facts.

His   "reason"
is   the   surface
of   a   deeper   instinct
digging toward form.

---

§17 – The Hidden Will Behind Logic

Logic   is   clean.
  It wears gloves.

But   the   hand   beneath
  is hungry.

Every   argument
is   a   path
worn   down
by a buried will.

Even   logic
has   a   scent—
the   scent   of
its creator.

---

§18 – Truth, the Tamer

We   train   ourselves
to   say   "true"
where it hurts less.

We   call   "error"
what   stings
our doctrine.

We   want   truth
to   behave.
We   want   it
to soothe.

But   truth
bares   its   teeth
when it is real.

---

§19 – The Philosopher's Secret Sacrifice

Behind   every   system
there is a cost.

What   did   he   silence
to make it whole?

What   gods
did   he   kill
to make it clean?

The   philosopher's   clarity
hides
the blood on the altar.

---

§20 – Dangerous Honesty

The   honest   thinker
is not polite.

He   does   not   seek   comfort
or consensus.

He   is   a   wound
that walks.

He   bleeds   insight—
and   leaves
a trail.

---

§21 – Physiology as Philosophy

What   if   we   judged
a   soul
by its laughter?

What   if   truth
were   not   a   concept
but a tone?

Perhaps   every   doctrine
is   a   digestive   system.
It   metabolizes
pain,   pride,
and pleasure.

Philosophy
is   not   mind
but   muscle.
Not   spirit
but gut.

---

§22 – The Will as Creator

The   world   is   not   read—
it is built.

We   see   what   we   will.
We will what we need.

The   philosopher
does   not   interpret   nature.
He   gives   it   a   voice—
his own.

§23 – The Future Philosopher

The next philosopher
will be a new breed.

He will not be a scholar.
He will be a creator.
He will risk himself
in every thought.

He will not seek
followers,
but fire.

He will know
that the truth
must be danced—
not defined.

§24 – On the Courage of the Free Spirit

To   be   free
is   not   to   be   safe.
It   is   to   feel
the   edge   of   truth
press against the skin.

The   free   spirit
has   unlearned   obedience.
He   walks   past   gods
with   a   smile—
not a prayer.

He   seeks
his   own   weather.
Even   storms
can warm him.

---

§25 – Skepticism with a Spine

The   free   spirit
does   not   destroy
from hate.

He   asks
because   he   sees.
He   sees
because he dares.

His   skepticism
is   not   fatigue.
It is flame.

---

§26 – Fear of Knowing

People   do   not   fear   lies.
They   fear
too much truth.

They   want
what soothes.

But   the   free   spirit
wants   to   burn.
He   wants
the   sharp   edge
of the real.

---

§27 – Quiet Distance

The   free   spirit
  does not shout.

He   steps   back.
  He   listens
  to silence.

He   knows
  that   noise
  is   often
  just fear.

---

§28 – Humor and Height

The   higher   you   rise,
  the more you laugh.

Not   out   of   mockery—
  but perspective.

To   climb
  is   to   see
  how   small
  the gods really were.

---

§29 – Thinkers and Taboos

The   deeper   the   thinker,
the   fewer   things
he finds sacred.

He   walks   where   others
build fences.

He   knows:
a   "no"   shouted   by   the   herd
is   often   a   "yes"
from the abyss.

---

§30 – Courage to Be Misunderstood

He   does   not   fear
to sound mad.

He   knows
madness   is   a   mask
for   truths
too   sharp
for calm ears.

The   crowd   will   mock
what   it   cannot   bear
to name.

---

§31 – The Air at Altitude

At   a   height,
  the air thins.

What   feeds   the   crowd
  does   not   nourish
  the   one
  who walks alone.

He   eats   less—
  but   he   tastes
  everything.

---

§32 – Philosophy of the Future

The   philosopher   of   the   future
  will   laugh
  where others kneel.

He   will   say:
  I   invent   myself
  in   each   decision.
  I   do   not   need
  to   be   right—
  only   true
  to   the   force
  that lives inside me.

§33 – The Reformer's Trap

The   reformer
  tries   to   save
  what needs to fall.

He   patches   holes
  in a sinking ship.

But   the   free   spirit
  lets   it   sink—
  and   dives
  toward deeper things.

---

§34 – Philosophy as Dangerous Taste

The   free   spirit
  cultivates   taste—
  not   in   art,
  but in life.

He   develops   a   tongue
  for   what   is   bitter
  and real.

Philosophy   begins
  where   instinct
  turns curious.

---

§35 – Deeply Buried Truths

What   matters
  does not shout.

It   sinks.
  It   waits.
  It becomes heavy.

The   deepest   truths
  must   be   lifted
  with silence.

---

§36 – Thoughts That Walk Alone

Some   thoughts
  have legs.

They   do   not   sit
  on   pages.
  They   wander
  with the thinker.

He   does   not   write   them.
He   lives   them—
and   watches
as   they   vanish
into the trees.

---

§37 – Dangerous Honesty (Again)

What   is   true
is not what pleases.

The   free   spirit
 asks   not
 what   is   useful,
 but   what   is   still   true
when no one watches.

---

§38 – The Spiral of Self

He   loops.
He   circles.
He   returns
to himself.

But   each   time
he is changed.

The   free   spirit
  spirals,
not   to   escape—
but   to   become
what   no   straight   path
could reach.

---

§39 – The Ascent is Cold

He   climbs.
  He   breathes   thin   air.
  He   loses   the   warmth
of old companions.

Above,
  there   is   clarity—
but less company.

That   is   the   price
  of altitude.

---

§40 – False Bridges

Between   truth   and   man
  stand   bridges—
  language,   morality,
  tradition.

The   free   spirit
  burns   them,
  then   walks
  the smoke.

---

§41 – The Smile of the Mask

He   wears   a   mask—
  but   the   smile
  is real.

Sometimes   he   hides
  to speak more clearly.

Behind   the   mask,
  a   silence
  sharper
  than speech.

---

§42 – Against Softness

Pity   dulls.
  Compassion sedates.

The   free   spirit
  feels   deeply—
  but does not sink.

He   lifts,
not   by   softening   the   pain,
but by naming it.

---

§43 – Danger of the Gentle

Beware
the   gentle   man
who never wounds.

His   peace
may   be
the death of truth.

The   truth   sometimes   cuts.
And   the   free   spirit
carries   a   blade
inside his breath.

---

§44 – Final Solitude

He   is   alone   now.
Not   from   exile—
but from altitude.

30

His   thoughts
echo
on empty peaks.

He   calls   out—
and   what   answers
is   not   a   voice,
but   the   wind
that   carries
his name.

§45 – Religion as Inversion

The religious man
turns the world upside down.

He sees weakness
and calls it strength.
He sees suffering
and calls it sacred.

This reversal
is not logic—
it is need.

---

§46 – Body-Hating Belief

The believer
distrusts the body.

He calls desire
a trap.
He makes sickness
a sign.

He worships
what does not pulse—

the   shadow
of   a   god
without blood.

---

§47 – The Guilt Machine

Religion   invents   sin—
so   it   can   offer
salvation.

It   teaches   you
to   tremble
before your own breath.

Then   sells   you
a   way
to be forgiven.

---

§48 – Power in the Priesthood

The   priest
knows the will to power.

He   does   not   lift
with   strength—
he   binds
with shame.

He   rules
not   with   force,
but   with   fear
of yourself.

---

§49 – Religion's Secret Hunger

Religion   wants   control.
But   it   hides
behind mercy.

Its   tenderness
is   strategy.
Its   peace
is pressure.

The   god   of   love
punishes
in a whisper.

---

§50 – Ghosts of the Past

The   religious   instinct
does   not   die—
it disguises itself.

Today,   it   speaks
of   science,   progress,
and humanity.

But   beneath   these   words
is   the   same   old   voice—
kneeling,
longing,
trembling
before the unseen.

---

§51 – The Soul as Invention

The   soul
was   created
to explain fear.

It   floats—
because   bodies
fail.

It   endures—
because   truth
was too heavy.

---

§52 – The Deepest Faith

Every   religion
  hides a wound.

What   the   believer
  loves   most
  is   not   his   god—
  but   the   pain
  that made him kneel.

He   believes
  because he bled.

---

§53 – The Philosopher's Piety

The   real   philosopher
  knows   reverence—
  but not for gods.

He   bows
  before becoming.

He   listens
  to   the   silence
  between stars.

His   piety
  is   not   submission.
  It is astonishment.

§63 – A Rule of Style

Style
  must live.

It   must   show
  not   what   is   said—
  but *who* speaks.

It   must
  bleed character.

---

§64 – What Can Be Danced

Only   what   can   be   danced
  is worth thinking.

A   thought
  that   cannot   move
  has already died.

---

§65 – Shadows in Truth

The   deepest   truths
  are half-shadows.

They   shimmer.
They   evade.
They seduce.

---

§66 – Wisdom's Smile

Wisdom
 is not solemn.

It   smiles—
 not   because   it   knows   everything,
 but because it no longer needs to.

---

§67 – Masks Again

Every   deep   thinker
 loves a mask.

Not   to   hide—
 but   to   reveal
 what   naked   truth
 never could.

---

§68 – Cold Insight

Some   truths
 can   only   be   seen
 when   the   heart
 goes quiet.

Warmth
 blurs the edge.

Coldness
 lets   the   outline
 cut.

---

§69 – Becoming is Better

Why crave arrival?

Becoming
 is   richer
 than being.

What   you   are
 can   die.
 What   you're   becoming
 lives.

---

§70 – Heavy Wings

A   great   mind
  has   wings—
  but   they   are   made
  of iron.

Flight   is   hard.
  The   air
  resists.

But   still
  he flies.

---

§71 – Morality as Weakness

When   people   call
  something   "moral,"
  they   often   mean
  they're   too   tired
  to oppose it.

---

§72 – The Soft Lie

We   lie
  not   to   deceive—
  but to soften.

The   truth
  is   sharp.
  We   pad   it
  for ourselves.

---

§73 – Truth and Women

Truth,
  like   a   woman,
  resists possession.

She   moves.
  She   smiles.
  She   disappears
  when claimed.

---

§74 – The Strong are Often Quiet

The   strongest   people
  do not assert.

They   act.
  They   change.
  They   pass—
  like   storms
  with   names

no   one   hears
until after.

---

§75 – Honesty as Violence

There   are   times
when   being   honest
is a kind of cruelty.

To   speak   plainly
is   to   unsheathe
a blade.

---

§76 – Deep Souls

A   deep   soul
does   not   swim
on   the   surface
of feeling.

It   dives.
It   does   not   always
rescue   others.
But   it   touches
what lies buried.

---

§77 – The New Nobility

The   new   nobility
  will not be of blood.

It   will   be   made
  of   restraint,
  taste,
  and
  self-overcoming.

They   will   rise
  not   by   conquering   others—
  but   by   mastering
  themselves.

---

§78 – The Heaviest Thought

To   know
  that   nothing   lasts—
  and   still
  to love it.

That
  is strength.

---

§79 – Little Vices

Great   men
  have little faults.

Tiny
  ugly
  human things.

That's   how   you   know
  they   aren't   gods—
  and   why
  they still shine.

---

§80 – Boredom in Heaven

If   gods   were   real,
  they'd be bored.

Perfection
  cannot   laugh.
  It cannot dance.

Even   angels
  would   long
  to stumble.

---

§81 – Praise is Poison

Praise
numbs   the   nerve
of the doer.

He   begins
to   act
for echoes.

Praise
steals
solitude.

---

§82 – The Most Dangerous Word

The   most   dangerous   word
is "should."

It   turns   dreams
into prisons.

It   wears
the   mask   of   duty—
but   breathes
resentment.

---

§83 – The Lightness of Truth

Not   all   truths
 must be heavy.

Some   truths
 sing.
 They   lift
 rather than crush.

Wisdom
 has wings too.

---

§84 – The Strong Do Not Shout

Force
 is quiet.

Only   the   brittle
 need   to   break   things
 to   prove
 they exist.

The   strong
 touch lightly.

---

§85 – Misunderstanding as Shield

To   be   misunderstood
  is   sometimes
  a gift.

Clarity
  is   dangerous
  to   those
  who   still   worship
  mirrors.

---

§86 – The Mirror Smiles

You   become
  what you watch.

And   if   you   look
  long   enough—
  the   mirror
  will   smile
  your   own   face
  back to you.

---

§87 – When One Forgets the Why

He   who   loses
  his   *why*

is   at   the   mercy
 of any *how*.

Even   strength
 grows   sick
 when   it   no   longer
 knows
 what it's for.

---

§88 – The Smile of Power

True   power
 rarely frowns.

It   smiles—
 not   out   of   kindness,
 but   from   knowing
 what others don't.

---

§89 – The Weight of the Small

Sometimes
 a   single   word
 crushes   more
 than a blow.

A   glance
  can   ruin
  a future.

Small   things
  fall   heavy
  in the right hands.

---

§90 – The Thinker's Debt

Every   deep   thought
  costs something.

It   borrows
  from   the   body.
  From   sleep.
  From peace.

The   soul   thinks—
  but   the   bones
  pay.

---

§91 – Wanting to Be Right

Wanting   to   be   right
  is   often
  just   fear

dressed   up
as logic.

Truth
rarely   cares
to win.

---

§92 – Love and Clarity

Love   needs
a little fog.

Too   much   clarity
freezes it.

The   truest   warmth
sometimes   comes
from   not   knowing
everything.

---

§93 – The Oldest Truth

The   oldest   truths
hide in silence.

Before   the   word—
there   was   rhythm.

Before   belief—

there was breath.

---

§94 – Knowing Too Soon

He   who   understands
 too   early
 misses   the   flavor
of confusion.

Wisdom
 needs   delay.
 It   ripens
through mistake.

---

§95 – The Dignity of Error

There   is   dignity
 in   being   wrong
 honestly.

A   true   mistake
 is   cleaner
than a correct lie.

---

§96 – Where You Cannot Go

Each   person
  has   a   thought
  they   fear
  to think.

Behind   that   wall
  waits
  the next world.

---

§97 – Slow Light

There   is   light
  that   comes   quickly—
  and   light
  that   takes   years
  to reach the eye.

The   brightest   thoughts
  are   often
  the slowest.

---

§98 – Trust the Rhythm

Even   when   thought
  fails,
  the   rhythm
  remains.

Follow   it—
and   the   mind
will return.

---

§99 – Thin Morality

Some   virtue
 is   just   fear
 wearing
 a nice hat.

---

§100 – Fire Beneath Ice

Stillness
 is   often
 where the fire burns.

Calm   people
 aren't   cold—
 they   burn
 inward.

---

§101 – Deep Time

Some   questions
 take

generations
to ask properly.

A   real   thought
is   planted
long   before
it's spoken.

---

§102 – Listening Beyond

To   listen
is   not   to   wait
for your turn to speak.

It   is
to   enter
another breath.

To   risk
not   returning
as the same.

---

§103 – No Thought Without Cost

Every   original   thought
destroys
a little peace.

Creation
  is   not   gentle.
  It   leaves
  a mark.

---

§104 – A Dangerous Kindness

Some   kindness
  binds.

It   flatters
  to tame.

The   gentlest   hand
  can   be
  a leash.

---

§105 – When Ideas Sleep

An   idea
  can   sleep
  for centuries.

But   when   it   wakes—
  the   world
  shakes.

---

§106 – The Quiet Ones

The	ones	who	seem
to		say	least
often			feel
the most.			

They			carry
more			truth
than		their	words
reveal.			

---

§107 – Love Without Reward

To	love
without	return—
without	recognition—
without applause—	

is divine.

Not	godly—
but	human
at its best.	

---

§108 – A Mind With a Past

The   soul
remembers
what the brain forgets.

Your   choices
echo
the   songs
you   never   learned
but always knew.

---

§109 – Politeness as Weapon

Manners
can maim.

The   right   smile
at   the   wrong   time
shuts   a   door
forever.

---

§110 – Living Over Arguing

He   who   argues
has   already   lost
some   part
of the truth.

What   matters
is   to   live
what   you   believe—
not prove it.

---

§111 – Against the Herd

A   man   alone
is not necessarily wrong.

The   crowd
does   not
equal the truth.

Consensus
is not clarity.

---

§112 – The Fruitful Wound

Some   wounds
bear fruit.

Pain,
when   faced,
plants   seeds
that comfort never knew.

---

§113 – The Final Smile

Sometimes
a   smile
is   the   last   mask
before silence.

What   looks   like   joy
may   be
resignation—
or release.

---

§114 – Depth Cannot Be Taught

No   teacher
can   give
depth.

You   can   hand   someone
a   shovel—
but   they   must   choose
to dig.

---

§115 – When the Flame Goes Quiet

The   greatest   fire
 burns
without sound.

No   smoke.
 No   flare.
 Just glow.

That
 is strength.

📑 *Part V: On the Natural History of Morals*

§186 – The First Instinct

The   moralist
 arrives late.

Long   after
 the   instinct   has   acted—
 he   builds
 a   cage
and calls it virtue.

The   body
 already knows.

---

§187 – Inverted Nobility

They once envied
the strong.

But they could not
become strong—
so they changed
what "good" means.

Now weakness
is holiness.
Now obedience
is the highest power.

---

§188 – The First Lie

The priest
was the first
great magician.

He told the people:
your instincts
are dirty.

Then he smiled—
and offered
a way
to be clean.

§189 – Resentment as Morality

They   didn't   forgive—
they forgot how to fight.

So   they   praised
humility.
Invented   sin.
Wrote   commandments
against joy.

And   called   it
conscience.

---

§190 – What Punishment Forgets

Punishment
pretends
to remember.

But   it   only   reenacts
the wound.

The   cause?
Forgotten.
The   meaning?
Invented.

§191 – The Birth of Justice

Justice
was   not   born
from fairness.

It   came
from   negotiation—
between   equal   forces
tired of bleeding.

It   was   a   pause,
not a principle.

---

§192 – The Debt of the Guilty

Guilt
begins
as a ledger.

"I   owe   you."
"I   wronged   you."
But   the   priest
turns it inward.

Now   you   owe
  yourself—
  forever.

---

§193 – Suffering as Currency

They   believed
  suffering
  could pay for sin.

So   they   built
  a   market
  where   pain
  bought purity.

But   the   seller
  was always the priest.

---

§194 – The Pleasure of Punishment

Cruelty
  was   not   hidden
  in early morality.

It   was   pleasure.
  It was performance.

The   whip
  sang.
The   crowd
  smiled.

---

§195 – Morality as Theater

Early   justice
  was   not   about   right.
  It was about spectacle.

Blood
  made   order   visible.
  Terror
  was the teacher.

---

§196 – Origin Myths Lie

People   want
  a moral origin.

They   dream
  of   a   time
  when things were pure.

But   beginnings
  are   savage—

and
is
disguise.

progress
often

---

§197 – The Animal Knows

We   are   animals
who   built
a mirror.

Then   we   called
what   we   saw
"conscience."

But   the   claws
are still there.

---

§198 – The Inward Turn

When   cruelty
was   outlawed,
it turned inward.

The   whip
became   guilt.
The   pain
became prayer.

§199 – Morality's Secret

Morality
 hates the body.

It   starves   it.
 Shames   it.
 Suspects
 every   joy
 with skin.

---

§200 – The Triumph of the Sick

The   sick
 have   found
 a   god
 who calls them blessed.

They   win
 by   weakness.
 Their   power
 is pity.

---

§201 – The Holy No

Asceticism
　is a holy "no."

No　　　　　　　to　　　　　　　the　　　　　　　earth.
　No　　　　　　　　　to　　　　　　　　　flesh.
　No to laughter.

This　　　　　　　　　　　　　　　"no"
　becomes　　　　　　　　　　sacred—
　and　　　　　　　　　　　　spreads
　like a shadow.

---

§202 – Seeds of a New Nobility

Not　　　　　　　all　　　　　　　morality
　is weakness.

Some　　　　　　　　　　　　　　men
　create　　　　their　　　　own　　　laws—
　like　　　　　　　　　　　artists,
　shaping
　their　　　　　　　　　　strength
　into form.

This
　is nobility.

---

§203 – The Future Spirit

We   need
  a stronger taste.

A   palate
  that   can   bear
  more   bitter   truth—
  and not spit it out.

A   freer   mind.
  A harder joy.

A   yes
  that   knows
  how to say no.

§204 – The Bookworm's Cage

The   scholar
does   not   hunt   truth.
He   hunts
safety.

He   dissects
what once lived.

He   replaces
wild   thought
with footnotes.

---

§205 – The Posture of Knowing

The   scholar
bends.

He   leans   in,
hunches   close,
lowers   his   head
to the book.

He   becomes
a tool.

Not   for   truth—
  but for facts.

---

§206 – Fear of the Heights

He   fears
  thinking that soars.

He   likes
  grounded   things—
  the   measured,
  the   cited,
  the safe.

What   cannot   be   proven
  frightens him.

---

§207 – The Philosopher's Solitude

The   true   philosopher
  walks alone.

He   does   not   gather   proofs.
  He gathers danger.

He   climbs
  to   places
  no one guards.

And   there,
  he listens.

---

§208 – The Connoisseur of Surfaces

The   scientist
  admires
  precision.

He   weighs.
  He   counts.
  He classifies.

But   he   forgets
  to   ask:
  what does it mean?

He   sees   the   tree—
  but   not   the   fire
  inside it.

---

§209 – The Philosopher Dares

The   philosopher
  is   not   content
  to name things.

He   steps
 into   danger—
 into question.

He   asks
 what   no   system
 can contain.

He   risks
 himself.

---

§210 – The Border Dispute

The   scholar
 maps.

The   philosopher
 crosses.

The   first
 draws   fences.
The   second
 tears them down.

They   will   never
 understand each other.

---

§211 – Instinct First

The   true   thinker
does   not   begin
with books.

He   begins
with   a   hunch—
a   tension
in   the   body,
a   rhythm
in the blood.

Then   thought
follows.

---

§212 – No School Produces Them

No   university
has   ever   made
a philosopher.

They   are   born
outside   the   fence—
in   open   weather,
under different stars.

You   can   teach
many   things.

But   not
what matters.

---

§213 – A Dangerous Flame

A   philosopher
  is   a   fire
  walking   in   the   shape
  of a man.

He   burns
  what   is   hollow.
  He   is   not   admired
  until he is gone.

And   even   then—
  only   by   those
  who still burn.

§214 – A Curious Kind of Honesty

We   moderns
 are   proud
of our honesty.

But   what   if
 it's just another pose?

A   way   to   stay   cold,
 to   avoid
 the   fire
of belief?

We   dissect
 what we fear to feel.

---

§215 – Tender Armor

We   pride   ourselves
 on being unchained.

But   even   we—
 free   spirits—
have scars.

A   certain   softness
creeps in.

We   grow   polite
where   we   once
burned.

---

§216 – Virtue's Shadow

Some   of   our   "virtues"
are   leftovers—
habits
from another age.

We   keep   them
not   out   of   faith,
but taste.

Like   keeping
an   old   sword
on the wall.

---

§217 – The Ache of Love

We   say
we   have   no   need
for love.

But   why   then
do   we   speak   of   it
so often?

There   is   pride
in   refusing   warmth—
but   also
a kind of frostbite.

---

§218 – Virtue as Style

Some   men
wear   their   virtues
like tailored coats.

Not   to   stay   warm—
but to be admired.

Their   decency
has   design.
Their   goodness
a signature.

---

§219 – The Fear Behind Kindness

Kindness
can   come
from cowardice.

It   avoids
conflict,
not   out   of   peace—
but   fear
of being seen.

---

§220 – The Quiet Will to Power

There   are   those
who   dominate
without   raising
their voices.

They   praise   others
to remain in control.

Their   humility
is strategy.

---

§221 – The False Light

Some   virtues
glow.

But   only   because
  they   burn
  something   else
  in secret.

What   feeds
  the brightness?

Look beneath.

---

§222 – The Passion for Truth

Why
  do   we   worship
  truth?

Is   it   courage—
  or   just
  a taste?

Some   seek   truth
  not   to   live   better,
  but   to   feel
  superior.

---

§223 – The Honest Instinct

There   are   people
who   tell   the   truth
not   because   they   choose—
but   because
they can't help it.

It's   not   virtue.
It's   habit.
A   rhythm
in their bones.

---

§224 – The Lie We Love

We   still   lie—
but   now
we feel bad about it.

Our   guilt
makes   us
modern.

It's   not   that
we're   more   honest.
Only   more
anxious.

---

§225 – The Mask of Truth

Every   truth
  wears a mask.

The   question   is:
  who chose it?

Sometimes
  we   reveal   a   truth
  just   to   hide
  a deeper one.

---

§226 – Truth Can Kill

Not   every   truth
  is   good
  for life.

Some   truths
  rot   the   root.
  They   stunt
  the   will.
  They   dry
  the soul.

There   are   truths
  that   should   come
  with warning labels.

---

§227 – The Delicate Artist

The   artist
 lies
 beautifully.

He   does   not
 report   the   world.
He   recreates   it—
 so we can bear it.

Art
 is   mercy
 disguised
 as vision.

---

§228 – Too Much Sunlight

Total   clarity
 can blind.

Too   much
 truth
 can kill joy.

A   mind
 needs   shadow
 as   well
 as flame.

§229 – The Mask That Heals

A   mask
 can   wound—
 but   it   can   also
 protect.

Sometimes
 truth   must   wait
 behind
 a kind illusion.

Until
 we're ready.

---

§230 – The Rarest Virtue

Some   speak
 the   truth
 like surgeons.

Others
 like dancers.

The   highest   honesty
 is   graceful—
 never cruel.

It   cuts
  without scarring.

---

§231 – Truth as a Style

We   don't   just   seek   truth.
  We shape it.

How   we   say   it
  matters.

There's   a   difference
  between
  a   scalpel
  and a poem.

Both   cut—
  but   only   one
  heals.

---

§232 – Life Beyond Illusion

Some   need   lies
  to live.

But   the   rarest   ones
  don't.

They   see
everything—
and   still
say yes.

That
is strength.

§233 – The Philosopher and the Flag

The   philosopher

does   not   wear

the   colors

of any nation.

He   is

his   own   flag—

waving   in   winds

that others fear.

He   belongs

to   no   homeland—

but to the earth.

---

§234 – What Is "German"?

German   spirit

loves   weight.

It   sinks

into systems.

It   believes
  depth
  means difficulty.

But   sometimes,
  depth
  is clarity.

---

§235 – The French Edge

The   French
  cut
  quick and clean.

They   admire
  wit,
  style,
  speed.

Even   their   seriousness
  wears perfume.

They   turn
  anguish
  into elegance.

---

§236 – The English Fog

The   English

  think   through

  mist.

Their   morals

  are   foggy—

  but familiar.

They   don't   analyze

  their   virtue.

  They assume it.

And   they   build

  empires

  on that feeling.

---

§237 – The Too-Civilized

We   have   grown

  polite.

Too   polite

  for genius.

We   clip

  the   wild   ones—

  file   down

  their teeth.

We   want
smoothness—
not greatness.

---

§238 – The Herd in Disguise

Modern   virtue
hides
a quiet conformity.

We   praise
what   won't
disturb us.

Every   "new   idea"
has   already
been approved.

We   celebrate
harmless rebels.

---

§239 – Dangerless Art

Art   today
is safe.

It   doesn't
risk

offense,
truth,
or transformation.

It   wants
applause
more than awe.

---

§240 – The Last Men's Anthem

We   grow   tired
even of greatness.

We   prefer
comfort.

We   prefer
consensus.

We   prefer
a   culture
that   asks   nothing
too deep.

We   are
almost done.

---

§241 – A Different Breed

Not   all
  are tired.

A   few
  grow   sharper
  in the quiet.

They   live
  like   wolves—
  apart,
  watchful.

Their   instinct
  still burns.

---

§242 – New Temples

What   they   build
  won't   look
  like churches.

Or   schools.
  Or palaces.

Their   greatness
  will   be
  in   what
  they refuse.

§243 – Free Spirits, Not Reactionaries

They do not want
the past.

Nor do they serve
the future.

They want
the real.

They want
to stand
without illusion—
and laugh.

---

§244 – The Sick Continent

Europe
is clever—
but tired.

It keeps moving
to stay upright.
It medicates
with opinions.
It hides

its   ache
 behind noise.

---

§245 – Beyond Nationalism

The   thinker
 must   break
 the spell of nations.

He   must   walk
 through   languages
 like rivers—

not   to   settle,
 but to cross.

His   loyalty
 is to thought.

---

§246 – The Philosopher of the Future

He   will   not   preach.
 He will not lead.

He will see.

And   in   seeing,
 he will overturn.

His   truths
will   not   comfort.
They will call.

He   will   not   fit
the   world—
but   the   world
may bend.

§247 – Beyond the Herd

The		noble		spirit
is rarely loud.				

He works
quietly,
without audience.

His				strength
is		not		shown—
it is held.				

He	does	not	prove	himself
by				shouting.
He		proves		himself
by lasting.				

---

§248 – Rank Is Felt

Nobility				
is		not		learned.
It is felt.				

A   noble   soul
  smells   disorder—
  and withdraws.

He   does   not   argue
  with   ugliness.
  He leaves it behind.

---

§249 – The Taste of Distance

What   is   noble
  knows distance.

It   does   not   mix
  without   reason.
  It   touches
  without merging.

Love
  without   confusion.
  Power
  without noise.

---

§250 – The Type That Doesn't Break

Some   souls
  bend.

Others
shatter.

But   the   noble   one
 absorbs
pressure
like mountain stone.

His   instincts
 are   aligned—
even under strain.

---

§251 – Rank Without Comparison

The   noble   soul
 does not compare.

He   doesn't   ask,
 "Am I better?"

He   simply   is—
 and acts.

His   virtue
 doesn't   depend
 on   the   failure
 of others.

---

§252 – No Need to Condemn

He   does   not
 hate
what is low.

He passes it by.

He   doesn't   need
 to moralize.

To   him,
 smallness
 is   simply
 not interesting.

---

§253 – Beyond Resentment

Moralists
 need enemies.

The   noble
 does not.

He   rises
 by   instinct—
 not revenge.

He   acts
  from   surplus—
  not lack.

---

§254 – The Dangerous Knower

The   true   philosopher
  is not safe.

He   goes
  where thinking burns.

He   speaks
  what   others
  only flinch from.

He   does   not   ask
  if   the   truth   is   useful—
  only
  if it is real.

---

§255 – Wisdom Is a Style

Philosophy
  is   not   just   thinking—
  it's taste.

A   philosopher
  has rhythm.

He   does   not   just
  understand;
he   dances
  his insight.

---

§256 – The Secret Within Truth

Not   all   truths
  should   be   told
  at once.

Truth
  has seasons.

The   deepest   truths
  must   ripen
  inside   a   soul
before they bloom.

A   wise   man
  doesn't   pull
  a   flower
before its time.

---

§257 – The Last Philosophers

They   catalog
  what others built.

They   archive
  what others dared.

Their   minds
  are   tidy,
  but tired.

They   write
  not   to   challenge,
  but to preserve.

---

§258 – The Spirit of the Founder

The   true   philosopher
  is a legislator.

He   sees
  what   no   law   covers—
  and   plants
  new laws.

He   doesn't
  guard
  a   tradition.

He   becomes
one.

---

§259 – A New Nobility

New   orders
  require new men.

Not   just   intellect—
  but instinct.

A   soul
  that   can   create
  values
  without   needing
  permission.

The   noble
  are   not   born
  into   rank.
  They   become
  rank itself.

---

§260 – The Soul That Creates

The   noble   soul
   doesn't   borrow
   its values.

It makes them.

It   doesn't   react—
   it radiates.

Even   in   silence,
   it   shapes
   the world.

---

§261 – Dangerous Joy

To   live   like   this
   is dangerous.

You   will   be   alone—
   misunderstood,
   feared.

But   the   noble   soul
   laughs.

Because   it   knows
   what it is.

---

§262 – Noble Solitude

He   walks
 without company.

Not   out   of   pride—
 but difference.

He   has
 no   herd.
 No echo.

He   is
 his own echo.

---

§263 – The Final Yes

In   the   end,
 the   noble   soul
 does not mourn.

He affirms.

He   looks   back
 and   says:
 "I would do it all again."

That
 is nobility.

Post-Translation Thoughts

Nietzsche is often read for what he says about morality, power, or truth. But those are not his subjects. They are the voices he throws—masks in a play, tensions in a score. Nietzsche does not *argue* for values; he performs the crisis of valuation. He is not a philosopher who writes well—he is a writer who uses philosophy to unsettle thought.

This translation was guided by that conviction: that Nietzsche is foremost a literary figure—a dramatist of language, irony, and contradiction. He should be read next to the aphorists and the Romantics, not just the ethicists and the metaphysicians. In this light, *Beyond Good and Evil* is not a treatise. It is a *gesture*, a *tone*, a *theatrical unmasking of the Western tradition*.

What emerges when Nietzsche is read this way?

- That he writes in the mode of infinite prelude, refusing finality.
- That his metaphors are not flourishes—they are structural, ontological devices.
- That his "we" and "you" are tools of seduction and destabilization, not authorial clarity.
- That the most faithful translation is not the most literal, but the one that preserves voice and irony, the rhythm of rupture.

Throughout this process, it became clear that Nietzsche does not want to define "beyond good and evil." He wants to show that every attempt to do so *reinstalls the system it claims to escape*. Instead, he disorients. He circles. He performs what it feels like to think when there is no metaphysical ground beneath your feet. That is his literary genius.

Many scholars treat Nietzsche as a stepping stone to later theory. But what if he was already complete—as an *artist* of philosophical collapse? What if his legacy isn't what we can derive from him, but what he denied us the comfort of concluding?

This translation does not explain Nietzsche. It walks beside him.

And in walking, it tries to preserve his highest virtue: the courage not to resolve.

www.ingramcontent.com/pod-product-compliance
Lightning Source LLC
Chambersburg PA
CBHW080207300326
41934CB00038B/3402

* 9 7 8 1 9 6 8 0 4 4 4 7 3 *